Christian Thoughts for Every Day of the Year

Christian Thoughts for Every Day of the Year

NATHAN HADDOCK

NATHAN HADDOCK BOOKS

Dedicated to my father, David Haddock 1938-2020

I hope you will benefit from the

thoughts I share in this book.

If so, please consider leaving

a review on Amazon because this

helps others decide if this is a good

book for them.

Please leave a review by searching

for the book on Amazon

and scrolling down to the review section;

I would so much appreciate this.

Contents

Introduction

Everyone needs a little inspiration from time to time

on their Christian journey.

I believe in brevity.

You don't need, or have time for, a sermon every day,

but it is good to have something of God to focus on.

I've been writing Christian Thoughts for over two decades now

that have encouraged, inspired and challenged

thousands of people around the world.

My prayer is that God would use these thoughts

in your life, in whatever way you need.

January

———————————

That which you think about, you plant.

That which you ponder, you allow to grow.

That which you dwell upon, you will harvest.

Take control of your thoughts, or they will take control of you.

For every unhelpful thought, a better thought is available to you.

Let us upgrade our thinking, by dwelling on the things of God.

———————————

God wants 100 percent commitment to Him.

He is not satisfied with the half-hearted, lukewarm, lip-service

that we give to him.

He doesn't want 10 percent or even 99 percent commitment;

He wants 100 percent.

After all, He didn't send His son to die for 10 percent

of our sins or even 99 percent.

We are completely forgiven in Christ.

3rd January

_____

This week we have so many tools available to us to use for the

glory of God.

We have tools of encouragement, faithfulness, love, compassion,

mercy, grace and kindness.

Will we choose to use them this week, or will we hide behind

the fortress of apathy, comfort, shyness, laziness or pride?

4th January

_____

It is almost impossible for us to comprehend anything outside

our human, worldly experience.

To try and understand a God who is eternal, who has always

existed and will always exist, is difficult.

To get our minds around a God who lives outside of time is far

from easy.

This is why Jesus broke into time to show us a glimpse of what

this God is like, how much He loves us and what He is

prepared to do for us.

If we look to Jesus, we will see God.

5th January

_____

Seek, and you will find.

Pray, and you will be answered.

Listen, and you will hear.

Give, and you will receive.

Lord, teach me to seek so that I may find you.

Teach me to pray so that I pray according to your will.

Help me to truly listen with great patience and perseverance so

that I hear your voice.

Let me give generously, not so that I receive but so that others

are blessed abundantly.

6th January

_____

We have all been given the gift of life, but do we truly live each

day, each week?

Pursue everything that brings life and brings others alive.

Speak life into people's lives.

Speak life into every situation.

Live life in all its fullness.

God gives us the gift of life and also brings us truly alive.

7th January

_____

God meets with us all in unique ways.

On the death of Lazarus, Martha needed reassurance and

answers; that is what Jesus gave her.

Mary, her sister, didn't need answers; she needed comfort and

an arm around her shoulder, and Jesus was there for her and

wept with her. One event, two individuals, two different needs,

two different responses from God.

What do you need God to be for you today?

8th January

_____

With every piece of information you are given, with every fact or

myth you hear about someone else, with every juicy piece of

gossip you are told, ask yourself three questions.

1. Will it glorify God more to pass it on, or will it glorify Him

more for the chain to stop with me?

2. Will it encourage or build up everyone involved if I pass it on,

or will it be most helpful if I keep it to myself?

3. Am I passing it on to serve God and help others, or am I

passing it on to make myself look better?

9th January

_____

Let people lead you to Jesus, but do not let people become

Jesus for you.

There are many great leaders, teachers, preachers and debaters

who will draw you closer to Jesus.

They will inspire you and set your faith alight, but do not put

your faith in them.

Do not make them your idol or the lynchpin of your faith.

Your faith in Christ cannot be dependent on them.

They may well let you down.

They may give in to temptation.

They may even turn their back on faith altogether.

Let people lead you to Jesus, but let Jesus always remain the

focus.

10th January

Today offers the opportunity for forgiveness for all your

wrongdoings.

It offers a fresh start.

Today offers the beginning of eternal life.

It offers the beginning of a life lived with a purpose; a life lived to

the fullest.

If you turn to follow Jesus, all this and so much more is open to

you.

It's not just the prospect of heaven when you die,

but the prospect of peace, joy, grace, mercy, fulfilment,

comfort, fellowship, purpose and wholeness as you live

day by day.

11th January

Happiness in our lives will come and go; it is not something that

we can control; it is very much dependent upon our external

circumstances.

However, there is a joy that can be found in God that can be a

constant reality in our lives.

This joy is not tossed about by the storms of life but is an anchor

or harbour for us in those storms.

It doesn't depend on external circumstances in life but depends

upon God and upon our understanding of what He thinks of us.

This joy is worth more than gold or silver and yet is a free gift

available to all.

12th January

_____

In Jesus' anger, he overturned the tables of the

money-changers because of their wickedness.

If Jesus were to come into your house, what would He overturn?

Would He overturn your television because it wastes the time of

people who could put their time to better use?

Would He, perhaps, overturn your computer because it leads its

users into all kinds of evil?

Would He overturn your bookshelves as a sign that you focus on

the wrong things?

Would He overturn your dining table because of it being a

source of gossip and unwise talk?

What parts of your house and life does Jesus need to shake-up

or overturn?

Will you let Him do it?

13th January

_____

There is a time to speak the truth in love, and there is a time to

keep quiet.

There is a time to praise and encourage, and there is a time to

give constructive critique.

There is a time to correct, and there is a time to let things slip by.

There is a time to sing praises, and there is a time to lament.

There is a time to shout of God's greatness, and there is a time

to whisper in God's ear.

May God grant us the wisdom to know the right time for all

these things and help us tame our tongue for His glory.

14th January

_____

Each of us has unique gifts and a unique ability to serve God in a

unique way.

We are not all a Moses, a Paul or a Joseph.

Some of us are a Mary, whilst others a Martha.

Some of us a Gideon and some a Sampson.

Whatever our role, it is important to God and to the body of the church.

None of us should exalt ourselves over others or even see the roles or gifts of others as better than ours.

15th January

_____

Creation speaks of the creativity of the creator.

From the very building blocks of life to the largest galaxies,

His creativity knows no bounds.

He is worthy of our praise, and His creation is worthy of our care.

16th January

_____

As a teenager, I had a Saturday job in a supermarket.

There used to be a sign in our staff room that said: "What extra do I need to do when an area inspection is coming up?"

The answer being "Nothing!"

The implication being that we should be on top of our game at all times, whether an inspection is due or not.

I guess the same is true for us.

One day, the day and hour unknown, Jesus will come back like a

thief in the night.

If we knew He was coming back next year, we might have a real

push to tell our friends about Him, read our Bible more, pray

with more fervour, help a few more old ladies across the

road, etc.

However, we should be on top of our game all the time,

regardless of whether Jesus is

coming back tomorrow or in a million years.

The truth is Jesus may not come back

tomorrow, but we may meet Him tomorrow.

We don't know when Jesus will return, and we don't know

when we will die.

Are we ready and prepared to meet Him?

17th January

_____

Our lives, our words and our actions, are a story unravelling

before the eyes of those we meet day by day.

It is an authentic story full of twists and turns, joys and

heartaches, successes and failures.

People won't judge our story by the storyline but by our character development.

How we act and how we react to our circumstances will speak more to people than the circumstances themselves.

Are our actions consistent with what we believe;

do our efforts portray our beliefs, do our deeds speak of love, grace,

mercy, faith, kindness, goodness, self-control, patience and so on?

Does our story speak of Christ, or is that a subplot that we keep well hidden?

If our neighbours or colleagues could write a tagline for our story, what would it be?

Would it make comfortable reading as you read it to Jesus?

18th January

————————————

Jesus will never let you down.

He is completely trustworthy.

However, let's be very clear about this, the church will let you down.

Your local church and individual Christians will let you

down.

The universal church will let you down through its decisions; it's

lack of action or for a whole host of other reasons.

We need to remember that although we, as Christians and

churches, represent Jesus Christ, we are not Christ.

We are imperfect, fallen and frail humans who constantly get

things wrong.

So, we need to remember not to judge Christ by His followers

and remember that Christ himself is worthy of our trust,

for He will never let us down.

19th January

_____

There is great power in openness and honesty.

When we reflect in this way, we can learn from our mistakes,

build on our successes and approach the future with a

renewed focus.

God will shine His light on areas which He wants us to reflect

and will help us every step of the way in order for us

to be transformed to be more like Him.

20th January

_____

The more of God's grace we have experienced and continue to

experience, the more grace we need to extend to others.

21st January

_____

You have heard it said that...

God will not give you more than you can handle.

At first glance, it sounds good.

Doesn't it?

But, not only is it not biblical, it's not true either!

God will always give us more than we can cope with.

God asks us to attempt the impossible!

God gives us more than we can cope with and then works with

us to get through it.

God gives us more than we can cope with and then gives us

friends, the church and family to help us out.

God gives us more than we can cope with to show us that

we are not God.

I'm personally glad God does give me more than I can handle

because, if He didn't, He probably wouldn't be able to give me much at all!

22nd January

————————————

As Christians, we are where the world meets Christ.

The world will see Him in our actions, attitudes, responses,

judgments, character, words, compassion, and love.

What will the world see of Christ in you today?

23rd January

————————————

Prayer enables us to build a relationship with God.

The more this relationship grows, the more we learn how to

pray.

The more we learn how to pray, the more God uses us and ou

prayers in His great plans.

The more God uses us, the more we desire to pray and grow our

relationship with Him.

24th January

———————————

We cannot earn God's favour or His blessing – it is given freely

because of His goodness, grace and unconditional love.

25th January

———————————

Jesus not only paid the price for all our wrongdoings on the

cross, He then went on to conquer death.

For those whose faith is in Christ, death is no more than a

doorway from the land of the dying to the land of the living.

26th January

———————————

There will be things today that God will want to do

through you and you alone.

We can have the privilege of partnering with Him to accomplish

His wonderful plans.

Will we set our sights on Him, be open to His nudges and be

willing to be and do what He requires?

27th January

There is a grief that only God can understand.

There is a pain that only Jesus can empathise with.

There is a sadness in which only the Holy Spirit can comfort us.

28th January

We are called to refrain from being judgemental, but we are

called to make wise judgements.

The difference is this;

being judgemental puts us above the person we are judging;

making wise judgements recognises that we are all in the same

boat but can help one another.

29th January

You cannot have the miracles of God without the suffering that

proceeds them.

Suffering presents the opportunity for God to move in wonder

and power.

30th January

_____

When we finally meet God face to face, all our struggles,

questions, and sufferings will pale into insignificance.

When we see God face to face, our response won't be to

question.

Our response won't be to rage, blame or argue.

Our response will simply be to worship.

31st January

_____

Celebrate life!

Be thankful for all that you have!

Mark and remember times of God's manifest presence.

Praise God for who He is and for what He has done for you.

Draw close to God as much as possible.

Seek His will and live it out. Be a good friend to those who need

one.

Treasure what is truly dear to you.

Celebrate life!

February

1st February

_____

One of the simplest truths of the Christian faith is that the

Christian life is often a paradox.

We need to give to receive; we need to die to truly live; we need

to be last to be first; we need to surrender in order

to be free, and so on.

It is a truth worth remembering and clinging to, for it is not

a truth that the world would teach us or have us believe.

2nd February

_____

With God, through Jesus, we start each day from a place of

victory!

3rd February

_____

You've heard it said,

"Hate the sin but love the sinner,"

but I believe that Jesus teaches us to love the sinner and

concentrate on dealing with the sin in our own lives.

If we focus less on the sins of others and more on eradicating

the sin in our own lives, we would be leading by example,

and the world would be a better place.

4th February

_____

Jesus took on the suffering that we deserved so that

we might have all the riches that He so rightly deserves.

5th February

_____

It is when we are honest about our weaknesses, our faults and

our failings that God can begin to build us into

something magnificent.

6th February

_____

May God be your first thought in the morning, your last thought at night, and may He guide all your thoughts in-between.

7th February

_____

Where does your heart lie?

Your heart is found where you have stored up your treasure.

So where is your treasure?

Is it found in the scroll of your degree, the title of your job,

the size of your wage packet?

Can you find it in the car you drive, the house you own,

or in the names you can drop?

Does it lie with your children, your family or your friends?

As important as these things may seem now,

they will all seem insignificant in the light of eternity.

Perhaps we need to store up more where rust and

fire cannot destroy?

8th February

_____

Some of us have great intelligence.

We can fill our heads with facts and acquire great knowledge.

However, true wisdom comes only from God.

9th February

———————————

We need to seek God for who He is and not just

for what He can do for us.

10th February

———————————

There are some things in this life that we will never understand.

However, there is nothing that we can't choose,

with the help of God, to accept.

There is much that we fail to accept that is detrimental to many

aspects of our lives and the lives of those we love.

Today I choose to acknowledge that God knows all

things and that I do not.

I choose to accept this fact and accept that I am not

able or meant to understand everything.

I accept that some things I find difficult are there for a reason,

and I choose to accept all things that God puts across my path.

11th February

Without a genuine fear (not deep respect or reverence, but fear)

of the Lord, we will never have the wisdom even to begin to

understand His grace, mercy and love.

12th February

The Christian journey is a journey in company.

We are not alone in this.

None of us finds it easy.

It's a struggle, but we are not alone in that struggle.

We're in it together, helping each other and receiving help.

Don't go it alone; you'll never make it.

13th February

God does not bless our lives because of our goodness,

but because of His grace.

14th February

————————

Jesus, fully human, suffered as we suffer.

Jesus, fully God, knew the reason why.

Jesus suffered for our salvation;

we share in that through our sufferings.

Our sufferings have purpose and reason even if we,

unlike Jesus, do not understand them.

15th February

————————

God's perfect judgement and His wrath are held back by

His extravagant mercy, but nothing can hold back

God's amazing love.

16th February

————————

As Christians in our faith journey, we need to move more and

more from believing in God to believing God.

We need to, not just believe in Him but, believe what He says.

We need to believe what He says about who He is

and about who we are.

We need to believe what He says about what He can do and

about what He says we can do.

We need to believe His promises for us.

We need to truly believe that all things are possible with God

and live in the light of that belief.

17th February

_____

Draw near to God, seek His will, listen for His voice,

discover His ways, dwell in His presence, be filled with His

Spirit and don't rush away – for the road is rough and the

journey hard.

Let us purposefully start from a position of strength,

not end up there as a last resort.

18th February

_____

Church is a place where we live with the tension of

disagreement, knowing that the bond that unites

us is far greater than anything that could divide us.

19th February

_____

We all need to constantly upgrade our image of God.

Although He never changes, what He wants to be for us will

constantly change according to our needs.

Our image of God will have more effect on our lives

than anything else.

20th February

_____

Blessed are those who go the extra mile.

Blessed are those who walk in when everyone else walks out.

Blessed are those who give, not expecting to receive

anything back.

Blessed are those who know you're not OK even when

you say you are.

Blessed are those who hear the nudges of God and act on them.

Blessed are those who put others first.

Blessed are those who sacrificially help others.

Blessed are those who pick up the pieces.

Blessed are those who see the problems of others

as an opportunity to serve.

Blessed are those who take stick because of their faith.

Blessed are those who are faithful to others despite everything.

Blessed are those who love unconditionally.

Blessed are we who know such people.

21st February

_____

Each day is full of choices.

We have the choice to apologise, or not.

We have the choice to forgive, or not.

We have the choice to think the best of people, or not.

We have the choice to encourage, or not.

We have the choice to make a positive difference, or not.

We have the choice to do what God would have us do, or not.

Lord, help us to make wise choices each and every day.

22nd February

_____

We all have people in our lives who will knock us, test us,

frustrate us, annoy us, push our buttons, hurt us, hate us,

and humiliate us.

However, God tells us that our fight is not

against flesh... so we have an option...

we can go it alone and let these people crush us,

break us, use us, make us sad, down, depressed or

we can stand with God and turn

everything into an opportunity.

Difficult people give us the opportunity to learn patience,

humility, restraint, compassion,

unconditional love, and kindness.

Difficult situations can help us in trusting God.

With God, every difficult person provides us with an opportunity

to grow and to show the Godly attributes of mercy and grace.

Don't let them get you down; let them get you growing!

23rd February

_____

It is not what we have done in the past that is important; it is

what Christ did for us in the past that is important.

24th February

_____

Being a Christian is not an easy option for the weak.

Being a Christian doesn't mean you're protected from pain

and the struggles of this life.

God doesn't give the Christian the promise of being carried

when things get tough; in fact Jesus promises that if we follow

Him, we will have troubles.

However, He does promise that He'll be with us always,

will never desert us and that, in the end, He'll welcome us home

into His heavenly Kingdom.

25th February

_____

When we can't see God's reason,

it is then that we have to trust His heart.

26th February

_____

We must always ensure that our worth is found in God,

not in what He asks us to do.

27th February

_____

In a faith full of mystery, we have the option to worry about it

and even fear it or to celebrate it.

The choice is yours.

28th February

_____

Unconditional love is really tough!

It means...

whoever you are, I will love you the same.

It means...

whatever you do, I will still love you the same.

It means...

No matter how I'm feeling, I will still love you the same.

29th February

_____

You don't get crucified for being a middle-of-the-road,

do-gooder who taught a moderate faith.

You get crucified for being radical in all you do, from being radically outspoken to being radically loving of all.

The same is true of persecution.

March

1st March

Jesus not only saved you from something, but He also saved you

for something.

You have a purpose and a mission to fulfil.

2nd March

There is a difference between what the Bible tells us God

can do and what the Spirit tells us God will do.

We need to be inspired by the first and wait and listen

for the second.

3rd March

Praying "in Jesus' name" is not about adding magic words

to the end of your prayers ("in Jesus' name Amen").

It is about discovering His will and praying that.

It is about praying the same thing that Jesus would.

When our will and the will of Jesus agree,

then we can pray in confidence, and God will

answer in power.

4th March

_____

If we are prepared to pray, we must also be

prepared to be the answer to that prayer.

5th March

_____

We can spend our days seeking love, position and approval,

or we can spend our days realising that we already have

all that from the one who really matters.

6th March

_____

Jesus came to show us that the Kingdom of God is at hand.

Our job is to bring that Kingdom to earth.

We must bring God's heavenly Kingdom to earth in all

that we do.

We must have Kingdom

values and a Kingdom focus.

7th March

————————————

There is actual strength in strongly disagreeing and

yet keeping a healthy respect for one another and

maintaining the bond of love and peace.

8th March

————————————

We must love as Christ did.

Not waiting for people to conform to our ways before

accepting them, but accepting and loving them

unconditionally right from the start.

If, in loving them unconditionally, we feel that they

could do with changing, in some way, for

their own good, we can use the most powerful

weapon available to us – prayer!

9th March

———————————

If we measure our wealth by our bank balance and our

possessions, we will always be poor.

If, however, we measure it by our family, friends and faith

and invest in these things, we will

be as rich as anyone on earth.

10th March

———————————

Any interaction with someone reveals, at most,

just the tip of the iceberg.

Everyone has a history.

Everyone has open wounds and deeper hurts.

We all struggle along the best we can;

some of us are better at putting on the mask of

"Everything is OK!"

The anger, rudeness, frustration vented at us may have

been festering for weeks and may

have deep roots.

Let's meet it with love, compassion and understanding

instead of adding fuel to the fire.

May God help us all.

11th March

———————————

Life can sometimes be a struggle.

The road can seem to be continually uphill.

The constant demands, pressures and worries

can be almost overwhelming.

However, the message of the Bible is this...

I am with you, and I will never leave you.

I know how you feel, and although this world is tough,

I have overcome this world.

Stick with me, and we will crack this thing together.

12th March

———————————

In God, you have an ally in all things good and right.

He is closer than a brother and will support you

every step of the way.

If you work with Him

and follow His plans, you will succeed.

13th March

———————————

God showers His gifts upon us.

It is our choice whether we unwrap them, identify them,

understand them, hone them, and

put them to the best possible use.

14th March

———————————

Who can measure the enormity of the love that

God has for us?

Who can comprehend its unconditional nature?

Can we really get our heads around the fact that God loves

us despite everything?

He loves us...

He truly loves us!

Let it sink in.

Take it to heart.

There is no escaping it.

Whoever we are, whatever we've done,

no matter how awful we think we are, God totally

and utterly loves us.

15th March

This week we will have opportunities to serve God

and to give Him the glory He deserves.

Are you open to grasping these opportunities and turning

your focus from the mundane and onto God?

16th March

Let's keep it simple here.

When all is said and done, Christianity is not about religion,

laws, rights and wrongs, manufactured traditions, attending church,

saying and doing the right things, being better

than others, being pure, or a whole host of other things

that we associate with it.

When everything is washed away,

it is all about a relationship.

A relationship with God through Jesus Christ is all we need.

The grace of God covers everything else.

Everything else is mere detail.

Without that relationship, we are nothing.

With it, we are truly alive – waiting to move from the land

of the dying to the land of the living.

17th March

_____

Decisions that you make today can have huge implications

on both your future and others.

Take time to check out your plans with God to

ensure you make the wisest decision possible.

18th March

_____

You did nothing to earn your birth.

In fact, you had nothing to do with it.

It was an unmerited, undeserved, unconditional gift.

The same is true of your salvation.

You can't earn it – it is totally down to the undeserved,

unwarranted, unconditional love,

mercy and grace of God.

19th March

_____

Christianity is not about being right or even about being good;

it is about being forgiven.

20th March

_____

How would your weekend plans change if you knew

Jesus was coming back on Monday?

21st March

_____

Trusting God is the beginning of making the impossible possible.

22nd March

_____

Today I will look to...

the power of God in my weakness

the peace of God in my fear

the majesty of God in my wretchedness

the grace of God in my wickedness

the abundance of God in my lack

the provision of God in my need

the security of God in my anxiousness

the wisdom of God in my stupidity

the mercy of God in my failings, and

the holiness of God in my humanity.

I know He will not let me down.

23rd March

_____

God is obsessed with life.

He is obsessed with your potential.

He is obsessed with you becoming all that you

were created to be.

He is for you all the way.

He is your number one supporter.

No one wants you to succeed more than He.

24th March

_____

Your heart is always open before God.

He knows of all your heart's desires, your heartaches,

and your motives.

Nothing is hidden from Him.

Where there is darkness, He will bring light.

Hide nothing from Him, for all you are doing is

fooling yourself.

He will not take your heart, but if you choose to give

it over to Him, He will work within it

for your good and His glory.

25th March

_____

You will never walk alone!

You may feel that God doesn't care, as the disciples may have

as Jesus lay sleeping in the boat.

You may feel that God is distant, as Joseph may have

done as he languished in jail.

You may believe God is dead, as Mary and the women did

as they made their way to the tomb.

However, God has promised that He will walk with us

and that He will never leave us.

Some promises are worth holding onto.

26th March

———————————

Everything we do today stems from what we truly believe.

If we believe in a loving God; if we believe Jesus is not only

our Saviour but the Saviour of the whole world;

if we believe that that is truly "Good News,"

how is that going to shape our day?

27th March

———————————

There are thoughts and feelings that we cannot even

begin to express, but which God hears clearly.

God hears the cries of our heart, the churnings of our gut-felt

anguish and the screams that no one else can hear.

28th March

————————

As Christians, we are all on a pilgrimage in this world.

We are journeying towards God and journeying towards

being more like Jesus.

We are on a pilgrimage together, walking side by side

with each other.

We are never alone.

God provides everything we need for the journey and

continues to guide us if we look to Him.

29th March

————————

Ever before us is the strong and certain hope that

Christ has conquered death.

There is no need to fear for the ones whose faith is in Christ,

for He has conquered death and overcome the world.

30th March

————————

We live in a world of, so-called, human rights and equality.

However, it is an idea that is flawed at its very root.

People don't really want equality or human rights;

they really just want to be able to do

what they want to do, no matter what.

They want equality when it suits them,

and they want human rights for others when it

doesn't impede their rights to do what they want to do.

Human rights can't work because one person's rights

will affect the rights of others and vica versa.

Does one person's right to practice freedom of speech

trump someone else's right not to be verbally spoken against?

The list of conflicts is endless.

Thankfully, God doesn't believe in human rights.

God believes in humans.

He believes in justice, mercy, grace, and unconditional love.

If our focus is our rights, we become selfish.

If our focus is God, we become other people-centred.

31st March

_____

When our time comes to step out of the boat or

publicly admit to following Christ, we will find ourselves

falling short unless we have disciplined ourselves

to turn to God in all circumstances.

April

_____

Unless our faith is anchored in the person of Jesus Christ himself

and not on the teachings of a particular church or preacher,

then the wind and waves of this world will eventually

sink our faith.

2nd April

_____

One of the greatest out-workings of love is to help someone

achieve the potential that God has placed within them.

3rd April

_____

We are wired to praise and worship God and give Him glory.

If we do not praise God, our beings will praise something else.

If it is not God that we worship,

we will begin to worship an idol or idols.

We will bow down at the altar of sport,

work, family, recreation or even ourselves.

To God, be all the glory.

4th April

———————————

Christianity is not a set of rules to follow, but a person

to get to know and trust.

Our salvation is not dependent on how we live but on how Jesus

lived, died, and conquered death.

It is not about us; it is all about Him.

5th April

———————————

If you have found the most precious gift that this life has to offer,

guard it with all you have, then share it with all you know.

It is in giving that we truly receive.

6th April

———————————

We are created in the image of God.

We need to be very careful not to create God in our image.

We must not limit God to our limitations of thought or speech.

We must continue to acknowledge His mystery, His immensity,

His complexity, His "unfathomableness," and His glory that

we can't even set our eyes upon.

In other words, we need to let God out of the box!

7th April

_____

God wrote Jesus into the story of human history, not as an

after-thought, but as the central character around whom every

other character and event revolves.

8th April

_____

God is continually drawing you to Himself.

You have the option of letting yourself be drawn near or

fighting against it and walking away.

9th April

_____

I can't give you anything that is not already yours.

I cannot bring you anything of any real goodness.

I have nothing with which to bargain with

I simply come.

I simply fall on your great mercy and grace.

I simply look to Jesus.

I simply look to Jesus to pay the price I owe.

I look to Him to take the punishment I deserve.

I trust that He with be my salvation.

I trust that He will speak on my behalf.

I come with nothing and yet hope for everything.

Knowing that He will never let me down.

10th April

_____

We are living in a period of Grace.

God is refraining from judging us and passing sentence

on the wrong that we do.

Instead, His grace and mercy flow like rivers over our lives.

He gives us wonderful things that we don't deserve and

prevents us from experiencing

much we deserve.

Thank you, Father, for your loving kindness that

provides grace and mercy in our lives.

11th April

———————————

Jesus doesn't talk about problems;

He talks about possibilities.

For each situation we face, Jesus provides us with possibilities

if we choose to look to Him for them.

12th April

———————————

We are all made in the image of God, and we are all loved

equally by God.

Therefore, we should always look for the best in others.

Celebrate the good in people.

Build others up, encourage them and only speak good of them.

After all, we all have enough faults of our own to be working on

without needing to point out the flaws of others.

13th April

On the seventh day, God rested from creating;

but He has never stopped sustaining.

14th April

The world says, earn it.

God says, have it.

The world says, strive for it.

God says, rest in me.

The world says, achieve.

God says, I love you no matter what you do or don't achieve.

The world says, do.

God says, be.

The world says, want.

God says, give.

The world says, you're worth it.

God says, you're worth far more than that!

15th April

New friends are a blessing from God; old friends are

a double blessing.

Friends who fire you up and draw you closer to God are one

of the greatest blessings God can give you.

Thank you, Father, for these kinds of people.

16th April

We live in a fallen, imperfect world where sin and

suffering abound.

Yet this is not our home; we are just travellers passing through.

We are camping en-route to our seven-star hotel.

Things are uncomfortable, but we have our destination in sight.

We need to keep going, help those around us, and make

the most of the journey.

Heaven is closer than you think.

17th April

_____

When you pray, God will hear you.

God loves to give you the desires of your heart.

However, God will only give you good things, things that

He knows, in His wisdom, will prosper you and be good

for you physically, mentally and spiritually.

Do not then expect God to provide for all your wants,

but do expect Him to provide for all your needs,

according to His amazing will.

18th April

_____

We often feel life is unfair.

We cry out for justice.

However, in truth, we don't really want it.

For if we want life to be fair and we want justice for murderers,

wife beaters and sexual predators, we also must demand

justice in our own lives.

We must also pay the penalty for what we have done.

So, in fact, we want justice on our own terms –

and that is no justice at all.

Perhaps we just need to say and trust, along with the

author of Genesis, –

"Will not the Judge of all the earth do right?"

19th April

_____

Our job is...

To be blessed so that we can be a blessing.

To be loved so that we can truly love others.

To receive so that we can give.

To learn so that we can teach.

To experience so that we can tell.

To become empty so that we can be filled.

To be weak so that we may become strong.

To explore so that we can lead.

To be so that others can see.

20th April

_____

It is very popular to train your body and even your mind,

but how about your Spirit?

When did you last train yourself to listen for that

small still voice?

When did you train yourself to come into God's presence?

When did you last fast or pray for a good period of time?

We worry and focus on that which will fade away,

but let us not forget that which will last forever.

21st April

————————

Words and actions, actions and words.

Words are not enough; they need to be backed up with actions.

Actions in of themselves can be meaningless unless the root

behind them is explained.

The Gospel needs to be explained in both words and actions –

one or the other is not enough.

The Gospel is a gospel of words, and those words put into action.

It is a gospel of "Do as I say and what I do."

We must tell people of the Good News, and we must

also be the Good News to others.

22nd April

_____

Life is not made up of the things that hold our attention

but of the person who holds us.

When you are in the loving grip of God, it is then that

life truly begins.

23rd April

_____

We love labels.

Don't we?

We love to call ourselves Doctor, Pastor, Apostle,

Prophet, Mr. Smith MP. F.R.G.S. B.Div. R.S.V.P.

We define ourselves by the work we do and the company

we keep.

We love to label people as intelligent, trustworthy, famous,

holy, respected, and so on.

However, what if people could see our real labels –

bitter, fearful, angry, back-biting, negative, lazy,

false, jealous, liar, guilty, fragile etc.

Do we use labels to hide behind, make us feel better

and raise our status?

If so, perhaps we should find comfort in the labels

that God would give us:

Forgiven

Son

Adopted

Worthy

Precious

Chosen

Loved

Fragrant

Special

Useful

Family

To Die For

Wanted

Beautiful

Wonderful

Spectacular

and the list goes on and on.

24th April

―――――――――

There are days when you do not need prayer or the Bible

to help you be more Christ-like.

God sends us people and circumstances to teach us patience,

kindness, love, endurance, grace, mercy, joy, gentleness,

and a whole host of other things.

God loves it when we read His Word and speak to Him,

but He never wants us to feel guilty

when we fail to do so and can teach us in many different ways.

25th April

―――――――――

God's mercy saves you from the worst punishment imaginable,

a punishment you fully deserve.

God's grace adopts you into His family and gives you all

wonders that that entails.

26th April

―――――――――

One of the most important things in life is to realise that God, and not you, is the most important thing in your life.

27th April

_____

With God, you have the potential for true greatness.

It may not necessarily be greatness as the world sees it,

but it is greatness nonetheless – and greatness

that will last and last.

28th April

_____

Do nothing for show or out of selfish motives.

Do not seek for yourself glory or thanks from others.

Do not think of yourself as better than anyone; instead,

be humble.

Yet, do not put yourself down.

See yourself in a correct light.

Live your life so that Jesus is on show.

Live so that no-one even questions your motives.

Make sure it is God who gets all the glory.

Always be of service to others and not just your friends.

Before God, be humble, and He will give you His light.

29th April

_____

We need to seek God each day with expectancy.

We have to raise our levels of faith and trust that He will

meet with us in new and exciting ways.

He stands there waiting with arms outstretched.

We need to grasp the nettle of faith and run towards Him.

30th April

_____

Life is tough, and the truth of the matter is that God doesn't

promise us an easier life.

God is real about it.

He doesn't give us false hope for this life, but genuine

hope for the life to come.

May

1st May

———————

Our job is not to judge but to honour people

and look for the best in them.

2nd May

———————

To be human is to suffer.

To be able to see the good in suffering is to

see a little piece of heaven on earth.

3rd May

———————

To God be the glory in all things;

In our waking and our sleeping;

In our doing and our being;

In triumphs and our failings;

In our busyness and our rest;

In our enjoyment and our boredom;

In our work and our play;

In our words and our silence;

In our good times and in our bad times;

To God be the glory in all things.

4th May

_____

They say that "where there is life, there is hope,":

but the message of Christianity is that

where there is death, there is an even greater hope.

5th May

_____

God asks us to reach for the impossible in order to

achieve the improbable so that His glory is undeniable.

6th May

_____

If God is good, and I believe Him to be so, then that is a constant.

He is not good at some points and bad at others.

He is not good when your life is going well and bad when

disaster strikes you.

God is good, no matter what.

If God is good all the time, He is worthy of our praise all the time.

He is worthy of our praise when things are going well for

us and worthy of our praise when disaster strikes us.

Will you choose to give God sacrificial praise

when things go wrong?

7th May

_____

If you show people what they are really like they will

shrivel up and even die a little.

However, if you show them what God thinks of them,

they will grow, bloom and bear fruit.

8th May

_____

There is no greater freedom than our

God-given freedom to choose.

Let us rejoice in it and use it with wisdom.

9th May

_____

Do not let the world define who you are.

The world will tell you that you are a teacher or an

accountant, or unemployed.

The world will say you are successful or a plodder or a failure

just because of the job you do or the

fact that you can't get a job.

The world will say you are single or married or separated or

divorced or widowed and again, will put you

in a box accordingly.

The world will judge you and put you in any number of boxes.

Let yourself, instead, be defined by God.

He knows you and treats you as an individual.

God sees you as you are and defines you as precious,

valued, special, loved, cherished, worthy, wonderful,

and magnificent.

He sees you as the apple of His eye.

He defines you as worthy of dying for.

He doesn't put you in boxes but releases you from them.

Let us see and define ourselves today

as God sees and defines us.

10th May

It's not about you, how good you are, how holy you are,

what you have done or even what you plan to do.

It's all about Jesus and what He has done for you.

We can do nothing to justify the sacrifice He made for us.

We simply need to put our trust in Him.

11th May

In a world of uncertainty, where the future hangs in the balance,

it is good to know the one who holds the scales.

12th May

When you say "Yes" to following Jesus and making Him the

Lord of your life, you become adopted into the family of God.

You receive everything that goes with that.

You receive all that Jesus has earned for himself and all He

earned for you upon the cross.

God puts a robe on your shoulders and a ring on your finger.

God kills the fattened calf for you and prepares you a feast.

You become God's very own son or daughter and receive

all the benefits that that entails.

One day you will live hand in hand with Him for all eternity.

Can you hear the party starting?

13th May

_____

The amazing thing about God's memory is not the amount

He can remember but the amount He chooses to forget!

When we confess, God chooses to remember our sins no more.

14th May

_____

No matter what we are facing at present, we all have so much

to be thankful for.

We so easily get consumed by our troubles that we miss

the multitude of blessings we receive from God and others daily.

Sometimes we just need to stop and take stock and offer up a

prayer of thanks for all we have and all that has been

given to us and done for us.

15th May

———————————

I've been visiting a lot of beaches recently.

Most of them have been littered with dead crabs.

Mainly reasonably small but a few bigger ones as well.

They can be found in the rock pools and along the tide-lines;

Hundreds and hundreds of dead crabs.

It was only yesterday when I visited a Marine Life Centre that

I found out that they were not dead crabs at all

but just the discarded shells of growing crabs.

Little did I know that crabs grow, move out of one shell

and grow another one

(along with any limbs they may have lost as well).

Isn't God's creation amazing?

What I had thought was death was actually growth and new life.

We do the same.

Don't we?

With friends and family, what we see as death is actually

growth and new life.

Just like the discarded shells of all those crabs,

our body is just a shell housing what is eternal.

If we are in Christ, there is no such thing as death;

we just discard what we don't need

anymore and move on to bigger and better things.

Isn't God's creation amazing?

16th May

_____

Just like looking at a bend in the road, none of us knows what

lies beyond into the future.

Yet, we have a tendency to worry and speculate about

what the future holds.

We spend our lives worrying about so many things

that never actually happen.

We worry so much about the if, buts and maybes of life

that we rob the present of much of its happiness.

Trust God with what lies ahead and live in the moment.

17th May

_____

There are things that take place in this life that we will

never understand.

We will never know the "why" of many situations.

However, we do have the opportunity to know the God who can

comprehend the answers and understand how we feel.

He tells us that our ways are not His ways;

what we would choose to happen is not,

necessarily, what He would choose to happen.

Our job is to trust that God's wisdom is far greater than ours.

18th May

———————————

Jesus wouldn't ask you to follow Him if He were not

going to welcome you into His glorious Kingdom.

19th May

———————————

We need to live for the moment, for that is the only place

God's grace exists.

His grace doesn't cover the worries of tomorrow or the regrets

of yesterday.

However, His grace is more than sufficient for us today.

20th May

_____

If you look, you will see the fingerprints of your creator all

around you.

They are there in the intricacies of the tiniest flower and in

the complexities of the human body.

You can see God's creative touch in the diversity of His creation,

and you can see God's

gentle touch in the subtle hues of a Spring morning.

His fingerprints surround us if we only

stop long enough to really see them.

21st May

_____

We have so much to be thankful for.

Today I am thankful for all those Christians down the ages who

have faithfully passed on the baton of Christianity so

that we can believe.

I am thankful for all those who have studied and translated

the bible so that we can read it in our mother tongue.

For all those who have gone against the odds and

continued to believe in extreme circumstances.

For those who brought Christianity to the shores of our country.

Thank you, Lord, for these people.

Please help us to be as faithful.

22nd May

_____

If you point out someone's faults, you are as likely to

cause damage as you are to do any good.

If, however, you point out their identity in Christ, they will

likely come to see their own faults and see them as at odds

with who they really are and who they want to be.

This way, they now have the motivation to change.

23rd May

_____

Moses was reluctant to do what God asked Him to do, but

eventually, he did it, and God was faithful.

When we do what God wants,

He shows up and moves in power.

God will never ask us to do something that

He will not give us all the tools to do.

24th May

_____

Relationships are life-giving.

God did not create us to be alone.

He created us to live in communities, to have

relationship with one another.

Relationships give fuel to our fire.

25th May

_____

Much of life's problems are a matter of perspective.

We can always find people who are worse off than us.

However, the best way is to see our problems from the

perspective of God's immense love, mercy and grace.

When we take our problems to God, we have a much clearer

perspective on them and also an avenue to resolving them.

26th May

_____

You and I are the church.

The church has left the building and lives in our homes, in our

workplaces, with our neighbours and colleagues.

The church is present and living everywhere that we go.

The church is active, alive and living in our community.

27th May

_____

Are we too comfortable as Christians in the West that we're

doing the Holy Spirit, the great comforter, out of a job?

If we are living comfortable lives, can we really be

said to be being effective for God?

28th May

_____

God knows all about you.

He knows all your secrets, all your

bad habits, all your wrongdoings.

There is nothing you can hide from God.

Yet He loves you all the same.

He accepts you exactly as you are.

You don't have to clean up and break those

bad habits before coming to God.

He will take you exactly as you are.

29th May

_____

It is possible to be devoted to the church and yet

not be devoted to Jesus and his teachings.

However, it is not possible to be devoted to Jesus

and not be devoted to the church.

In fact, if you are devoted to Jesus, you are the church.

30th May

_____

As the Good Shepherd, Jesus leads us

when we listen to His voice.

As sheep, we must learn to hear and

recognise the voice of Jesus.

When He leads us, He goes before us to prepare the way

and continually checks that we don't lag behind.

His whole job is focussed on guiding, protecting and feeding us.

What better place to be than with Jesus?

31st May

_____

When in difficult circumstances, Jesus is as likely to

change you as He is your circumstances.

June

_____

God's grace is not only sufficient; it is

outrageous, overwhelming, extravagant,

never-ending and all-encompassing.

More than that is it freely given,

undeserved and unreserved.

All we have to do is ask!

2nd June

_____

Happiness is totally dependent on your circumstances,

whereas there is a joy that comes

from God that nothing can take away.

3rd June

_____

Who is there like Jesus Christ?

A man, fully human and yet fully divine.

A man without sin who freely gave up His life

and became sin for our salvation.

A man who is our saviour and yet wants us to be His friend.

A man who only requires our trust in order for us to

inherit all the riches that He has won for us.

Who is there like Jesus Christ?

4th June

———————————

To put God into a box is to deform

and misunderstand His reality.

To celebrate the mystery that is God is to bring Him glory.

5th June

———————————

If we live in the light and Biblical truth that, once saved,

we are saints.

We are far more likely to live Christ-like lives than if we live with

the false assumption that we are still just miserable sinners.

When you see your life as God sees it,

your whole life can be changed around.

6th June

_____

When Jesus invites us to follow Him,

He offers us a wonderful life where every tear is

wiped away, and no mourning will take place.

However, that is all to come.

When Jesus asks us to follow Him, He gives it to us straight.

If you follow me, you will have troubles.

You will be persecuted.

Becoming a Christian doesn't mean your life will suddenly

become simple, sorted and wonderful,

but it does mean you will have Jesus with you

every step of the way.

It also means we do have the promise of a tough life

but with a wonderful pension plan!

7th June

_____

When we do what is good, right, honourable, true, holy,

and Godly, we bring a little bit of heaven down to earth.

In doing such things, we answer our own prayer of

"On earth as in heaven."

8th June

_____

No-one is outside of God's unfailing,

unfathomable and unconditional love.

No matter who you are or what you have done,

God loves you.

There is nothing that you can do that will make

you deserve that love, but there is nothing that you can

do that will cut you off from that love.

9th June

_____

We live in a broken world.

We live in a fallen world.

Things are not meant to be this way.

We have to keep reminding ourselves

that this is just temporary.

This is not our home.

We are just passing through.

Heaven is waiting!

10th June

———————————

Sometimes you will find that you just don't have

the words to say when you pray.

It is in those times that God easily interprets our cries,

our screams, our sighs, our tears, our

squeals of frustration and even our silence.

Turn your focus to God

because He always hears you.

11th June

———————————

God is love, and everything He does flows from that.

In Him is no evil.

Everything He does is good.

Trust Him to do good by you this day.

12th June

———————————

If you are barely hanging on,

perhaps it is time to let go and let God.

God's power is most evident in our weakness.

13th June

_____

If your life contains a deep relationship with Jesus Christ,

you can weather any storm and still not be

afraid of the storm clouds on the horizon.

14th June

_____

We have a choice each day to build people up

or put them down.

We can choose to be a force for good in the lives of those

around us or not to be.

We can decide whether our words will injure or heal.

What will you choose to do today?

15th June

———————————

God's goodness shown to us has nothing to do with our

goodness or how much we deserve it, but

everything to do with His love and grace.

16th June

———————————

God and Man a Shocking Tale

If you live in a world of child sacrifice

where you'd do anything to appease the gods

there's a shocking story to be told.

It is a story that, centuries later, still continues to shock.

It's a story of a man and his only son –

his long-awaited son.

It's a story of a god who asks much of this man,

a god who asks for the most precious thing –

the most precious thing that this man had

and yet this man asked no questions.

He doesn't ask why.

He doesn't ask where.

For this god was asking for the sacrifice of his son –

this man's only son.

And this man doesn't question it at all.

Why was that?

Why did he not question this outrageous request?

Or was it not such an outrageous request?

In a culture where people had to give more and more –

had to provide more and more to appease these gods.

They had given their crops and their livestock.

They had shed their own blood.

Shed their own blood as a sign of worship.

They had cut off parts of their body.

They had dismembered themselves as a sign of devotion.

What else was there to give?

What else could be sacrificed?

Sacrificed so that the gods would show them favour?

So they took their firstborn,

they took the most precious thing they had,

and they offered them to the gods.

They took flesh of their flesh;

and bone of their bone;

and on the altars to unknown gods,

they gave up their children.

Gave them up in the hope of some favour.

Gave them up in their thousands.

Gave them up in desperation.

Sacrificed them.

Killed them.

In acts of violence.

In acts of violence, to please their gods.

So, within that culture of sacrifice,

it was not surprising that Abraham never questioned.

He never questioned God.

A god who, for the first time in history,

for the very first time, asked.

Personally asked.

Spoke to Him and asked.

Asked for this sacrifice.

For the ultimate sacrifice.

The sacrifice of Abraham's only child.

And so this shocking story unfolds.

A story that would have shocked.

Shocked all who would have heard it.

In a world of unknown gods,

One god had spoken.

In a world of uncertainty,

One god of certainty had been clear.

A god clearly stated what He desired.

A god had broken into human experience.

A god had asked for child sacrifice.

A god had asked Abraham,

asked him to give up his son.

And so, Abraham never questioned.

He went, and he took his son.

Took him to a place,

A place that would have been known to all,

known to all as a place,

a place for the sacrifice of children.

Shocking that a god would be so clear.

That a god would personally ask.

Ask so clearly.

For the first time in history

someone knew what a god expected;

What was expected of him.

What he had to do to please God.

And yet, there was a twist.

The real shock was yet to come.

The sacrifice of a child.

The most precious thing he had.

What was the shock in that?

This was commonplace.

This was just a step in the process,

the process of appeasing the gods.

No, this would cause no shock.

The shock was yet to come.

There on the mountain,

there in the place that everyone knew.

There in the place where children were brought,

where they were brought to die.

Abraham prepared to do something;

Something that he knew God had asked for.

There, he was to sacrifice his son;

his only son.

And then the twist hits home.

The real shock takes place.

God speaks again.

As the knife was raised.

As the sacrificial act began,

God stayed the hand of Abraham.

God spoke again

and stopped the act.

He stopped the act and then provided.

He saved the son

and in his place,

provided a ram.

What a shock that would have been

that God did not require his son.

That God did not require that which was most dear to him.

That God provided all He required.

So, God had spoken.

What a shock.

God had stopped the sacrifice.

The shock extends,

and God had provided,

provided all that was needed.

The shock was complete.

A shocking tale of sacrifice,

of God and man,

and God's provision.

Of God speaking into life

and turning things upon their head.

God saved the life of Isaac.

He saved Abraham's precious son.

And as numerous as the stars,

and grains of sand upon a beach

will be their descendants.

And of those descendants,

you are one.

17th June

_____

For the Christian, death should hold no fear,

for we know the one who has died

and come back to life.

Jesus has conquered the power of death;

we no longer move from life to death,

but from life to an even greater life.

18th June

_____

If you have faith in Him, God will call you

If God calls you, He will gift you

If He gifts you, He will use you

If He uses you, your faith in Him will increase.

19th June

———————

God should not be your last resort;

He should be your very first thought.

20th June

———————

Prayer, with a little faith, is a most powerful thing.

21st June

———————

Does the blame lie with us?

Our news is full of dreadful stories:

Bombings, suicides, murders, and fires.

It is easy to point the finger at individuals:

the unstable, the truly evil, extremists, and activists,

but are we not all to blame.

Have we pushed people away that much?

Have we neglected the lonely and the desperate?

Have we caused such ferocious anger in others?

Has our greed and arrogance pushed

people to this drastic action?

We do not feed the poor,

yet we are surprised when they steal to feed their family.

We have abundance, yet half the world has but scraps.

Can we really be shocked when they rise up against us?

We neglect to care for those around us.

Can we not understand when people crack

and do horrific things?

Have we abandoned all that is good

and exchanged it for a false reality of rights?

We have made our own rules by which we all fail to abide.

We cry out and blame individuals.

We cry out and blame God,

yet we have thrown God out and all His ways.

We have forbidden Him in our schools and workplaces.

We have taken His wisdom from our laws.

We have made money, intellect and selfish desires our God.

And now, do we reap the consequences?

Have our broken homes created broken lives?

Have our fragmented communities led to desperation?

Have our sinful desires been at the expense of others?

Have our grey churches created sceptical onlookers?

We have abandoned God.

Has God honoured us and given us the desires of our hearts?

Has He left us to our own vices?

Have we finally got it all our own way?

22nd June

_____

Do you have a plan for your life?

Do you know where you are headed?

Do you know your final destination?

God says that He knows the plans He has for us.

He says that they are good plans, plans to prosper us.

Jesus said that He is preparing a place for us.

A place where there will be no more death

or mourning or crying or pain.

Our job is simply to seek God for those plans and follow them.

Will you spend time today seeking God?

23rd June

_____

Suppose God answered all your prayers in the way

that you wanted Him to.

Would the world be a better place because of them?

24th June

————————————

Worry says that you are not trusting God to be all-powerful,

ever-present and capable of

overcoming any and every situation you face.

25th June

————————————

Jesus Christ is not just a source of hope; He is our only hope.

If we place our hope in anything else,

it will be found to be false hope and will let us down.

26th June

————————————

It's OK to have doubts.

Thomas had doubts,

but he took those doubts and worked them through.

He took those doubts straight to Jesus,

and Jesus allayed his fears.

We need to do exactly the same.

If we live with these doubts, they will eat away at our faith.

If we take them to Jesus, He will help us put them to rest.

27th June

———————————

God's blessings come in many different guises.

Some we see straight away;

some we only see and appreciate in retrospect.

28th June

———————————

Whatever you give time to in your thought process,

you give power to in your life.

29th June

———————————

To be a Christian, a follower of Christ,

you must follow all of His teachings.

You cannot choose those you like and reject those

that don't sit well with you.

In doing that, you are not following Him as the Son of God

and Saviour but simply as a good teacher.

In reality, you have to accept the whole package,

even the bits you might struggle with.

30th June

———————————

Can you see the fruit of faith in your life?

If not, perhaps you need to take a look at the soil

you are planted in, the things you are

being fed, the climate you are residing in,

or maybe it's even time for a bit of pruning.

July

———————————

We must speak the truth.

However, if we speak that truth without love,

in the fullest possible sense, then it makes

that truth all but meaningless.

2nd July

———————————

Imagine a world where we only received

that for which we were truly thankful?

We have so much to be thankful for.

Let us always remember to thank God

for all that He so freely gives us each day.

3rd July

———————————

No matter how far we have fallen, God is there to break our fall,

pick us up, dust us off and set us on the right path again.

4th July

_____

It is easy to love those we like, those who love us,

and those who agree with us.

However, God calls us to love everyone;

to love those who we find difficult;

to love those who wind us up and

do and say things we disagree with.

God calls us to love the unlovely, the disliked, the different.

Thankfully, the only way we can

do that is by His Spirit.

We can only do it by accepting love from

God and passing it on to others.

God longs to pour out His love upon you,

are you willing to accept it and pass it on?

5th July

_____

We do not need to defend our faith.

If Christianity is true, it needs no defence.

If it is not true, there is no defence.

The same is true of our actions; if they are right,

then we do not need to defend them.

If they are wrong, then there is no defence for them.

6th July

————————————

Prayer has the ability to lift yourself above your problems

and seek a heavenly solution.

7th July

————————————

If you truly want to see what is in a person's heart,

look at what they spend their money on and their time doing.

So, what is in your heart?

Remember, God searches the heart;

He knows what is in there more than we do ourselves.

8th July

————————————

Are the poor in our world really just

those who are starving or have no money?

What about those who are lonely

and are poor in friends and company?

The fearful who are poor in peace and security?

The exploited who are poor in justice and a voice?

The unhappy who are poor in joy and laughter?

The miserable who are poor in hope and happiness?

Like the financially poor, the answer is not to throw

money at the situation but to spread understanding

in real ways to help in the long-term.

Jesus came to bring understanding and to help us fight

for all who are poor in our world.

Will you listen to His teachings and join in the

real fight against poverty of all kinds?

9th July

_____

Just as Jesus healed the same illnesses in different ways,

so God meets us all at our very own differing points of need,

and deals with us as individuals in individual ways.

10th July

———————

God didn't need Moses to part the Red Sea

or the young boy to feed the five thousand.

He chose to involve them in His plans.

He will involve you as well if you make yourself available to Him.

11th July

———————

As Christians, we are called to forgive.

However, we are not always called to continue to stay

in the firing line that required

the forgiveness in the first place.

12th July

———————

Christian faith is not blind faith.

Christian faith is discovering the map and trusting

that when you reach the fold, the road

will continue and will take you home.

13th July

God's Law shows us that none of us will ever be good enough.

God's grace shows us that none of us will ever be bad enough.

14th July

There are small things that you can do today,

with God's help, that will change the lives of

those around you forever.

It might be a simple smile to someone feeling unloved

or hopeless or a helping hand to someone struggling.

Small gestures with God make huge

differences with echoes into eternity.

Will you bring a little piece of heaven to earth today?

15th July

When we make ourselves available to God,

He will use us in His plans.

When we get involved in God's plans,

then we know things will be good,

have purpose and bring glory to His name.

For God knows the plans He has for us,

and they are good and worthwhile plans.

16th July

––––––––––––––––––

Would you get on a plane not knowing where it is going?

Would you walk around in the dark not

knowing where your feet are landing?

Most of us wander through life without

really exploring where we are headed?

Have you really considered what this life is all about

and whether there is more to life than this?

Have you planned your exit strategy?

You might have life insurance and a will,

but have you insured where you are

headed at the end of the day?

17th July

_____

That which you receive from God,

be it money, blessings, wisdom, peace or whatever,

pass on to those around you.

Be a channel for God to your community, church, family,

workplace, friends, neighbours and whoever you meet.

18th July

_____

Becoming a Christian isn't about putting

all your troubles behind you.

It is about putting your troubles well and truly in front of you

but marching headlong into them knowing you have a

guide, a purpose and an all competent friend by your side.

Jesus makes it very clear that we will have troubles,

but that He has already overcome them –

even the troubling matter of death!

19th July

———————————

Will not God in all his wisdom and being just, do what is right?

When life seems unfair, and God seems distant,

we must trust that He who is entirely

trustworthy will keep all His promises.

20th July

———————————

Who, like God, loves you unconditionally,

undeservedly, unreservedly and unceasingly?

21st July

———————————

Never pray more in hope than in faith.

22nd July

———————————

Ask not what the church can do for you,

but what Jesus, through you, can do for your church.

23rd July

————————————

The local church should not be like a cruise liner

where you have a captain, a crew, and

everyone else is just along for the ride.

It should be far more like a battlecruiser or a fishing trawler

where everyone has a role to play in the ship running smoothly.

Every member of the church has a vital part to play

in furthering God's kingdom here on earth.

24th July

————————————

God overflows with love, grace and mercy.

God does not give to each of us according to what we deserve.

What He gives to us does not reflect our goodness.

What He holds from us does not reflect our badness.

God is a God who longs to give us,

His children, good and life-giving things.

25th July

It is very hard to sincerely pray for someone

and yet harbour ill will towards them.

Finding someone difficult?

Pray good things for them.

Find yourself with an enemy?

Pray for them – you'll soon find that after a while,

they are no longer your enemy, no matter

what they continue to do to you.

26th July

Eternal life is not something we inherit when we die;

eternal life begins the second we believe.

Once we believe it is an ever-present reality,

we have moved from death to life!

27th July

_____

When you make plans, always be attentive to letting

God interrupt you and change them at any time.

28th July

_____

When you are going through a difficult time,

God is far more likely to change you than your

circumstances.

29th July

_____

When you do good or do what is right,

and only God and you know about it,

He will honour your actions.

What greater reward could you desire?

30th July

———————

Never exchange being right for being light.

31st July

———————

When someone begs you for mercy

in fear and with true repentance

and your heart responds with love and compassion,

you get a brief glimpse into the heart of God.

August

_____

Every person we meet, who we help, who we smile at,

who we serve, who we listen to, who

we protect, who we feed, who we comfort,

who we give to, is Jesus in disguise.

Every person we hurt, who we are impatient with,

who we are rude to, who we lose our

temper with, who we scowl at, who we treat with disrespect,

who we have no time for, is Jesus in disguise.

We have the choice to pour expensive perfume on his head

or bang a rusty nail into His hand.

2nd August

_____

Our works cannot earn us salvation

or even favour in the eyes of God.

All our works should be done in response to the thankfulness

we feel because of what God has done for us.

3rd August

_____

In thinking less of ourselves than we should, we are,

in fact, thinking less of God in whose image we are created.

4th August

_____

Love is more important than being right;

love is more important than being successful;

love is more important than justifying yourself;

it is more important than being treated correctly.

Nothing is more important than love.

God is love, and nothing is more important than that.

Let nothing we do stand in the way of love.

5th August

_____

There is a time to speak out

and a time to hold your tongue.

There is a time to leap into action

and a time for thoughtful consideration.

There is a time to give answers

and a time to keep your own counsel.

The real wisdom lies in knowing which is which.

Lord, reveal to us your wisdom to know how

best to respond in every given situation.

Help us not be wise in our own eyes but

always look to you for the best way forward.

Amen.

6th August

_____

You cannot create an intellectual argument

to bring people to a faith in God.

It is the Holy Spirit who will draw people

to faith in the Father through the Son.

An intellectual argument (on its own) will simply

bring people to faith in their own intellect.

7th August

Jesus came to the weak and those of little earthly wisdom,

not because they were easily fooled but because belief in God

depends not on intellectual ability but the simplicity of

trust.

8th August

Today, forgetting all that is past,

if you humble yourself in true repentance,

you are given a clean start.

9th August

Today is the beginning of a whole new

chapter of adventure in your life.

You have the choice to grab it with both hands

and make the most of it or to let it slip past you.

You have a world of opportunity waiting to be discovered;

a pathway to plot a brighter future with God.

You are surrounded by people wanting to help

in any way they can, and you have God

wanting to guide you and wanting the very best

for you in all circumstances.

So, what are you going to do today?

10th August

_____

Prayer works best when our mind

and that of Christ are in one accord.

11th August

_____

The world is deaf to the Good News of Jesus Christ,

His saving power, His unconditional love, and grace.

This doesn't mean we have to shout;

it means we have to show them.

12th August

———————————

When we discipline ourselves

and take every thought captive to Christ,

then there is no room for fear and worry in our lives.

When we shine the light of Christ onto our thoughts,

we can see which ones are helpful and which are hurtful.

When we open our lives to Christ, it is we who benefit!

13th August

———————————

The same sun that melts wax, hardens clay.

Will you become malleable, yielding, mould-able

and soft-hearted, or will you be impenetrable,

inflexible, unyielding, hard-hearted?

Will you allow God to melt your heart or harden it?

14th August

———————————

God has placed in us the potential for greatness.

Will you seek it out, unlock it, grow it, develop it?

Will you use what you have been given

for greatness or for great gain?

Will you use this opportunity for God's glory

or your own gratification?

The choice is yours.

15th August

———————————

Will you join me in praying for and calling the church to put

what is important and central to the Christian faith

back in the centre?

At its core, the Christian faith is not about the issues of

a homosexual lifestyle or the sanctity of marriage;

it's not about the right to wear a cross around your neck

or on your lapel;

it's not about issues of abortion, the right to die, cloning, etc.

These issues, important as they may be,

deflect us from the central focus of the Christian faith.

Unless we, as the church, show the world

that the core of the Christian faith is

LOVE, GRACE, MERCY, HOPE,

FORGIVENESS, FREEDOM and RESTORATION

found in the person of Jesus Christ,

then we are failing those around us

and falling short of our calling.

Let us get back to what is vitally important before it is too late.

16th August

_____

There is a holy discontent that keeps us wanting

more of what God has to offer.

More of you, Lord and less of us.

There is a holy discontent that keeps us striving for

bigger and better things for the Lord.

More glory for you, Lord and less for us.

17th August

_____

We owe it to Christ to be Christ to all those around us.

We owe it to all those around us to show them Christ!

18th August

_____

God will relentlessly pursue you with His love.

He will extravagantly overwhelm you with His grace.

He will consistently surround you with His presence.

19th August

_____

There is a hunger only God can satisfy

and a thirst only God can quench.

We may and will try other avenues,

but until we realise that God is the answer,

we will remain hungry and thirsty forever.

20th August

_____

A friend of mine asked me to pray for her this week.

She had a job interview and really wanted the job.

I prayed for her, and she got the job!

Do I have a hotline to God?

Did I persuade God that she should get the job?

Does God do all that I ask?

No, but occasionally God does let us play a part

in what He is doing in this world if we only ask.

21st August

_____

Life isn't fair!

However, isn't that a positive thing?

God isn't fair; He doesn't give us what we deserve.

He doesn't give us the punishment

that our wrongdoings deserve.

Instead, He shows us immeasurable mercy.

In fact, He gives us that which we really do not deserve.

He lavishes upon us grace and favour.

Life isn't fair, but personally, I wouldn't have it any other way.

22nd August

_____

Colour, texture, sound, seasons, tastes, smells

and a multitude of other things for our enjoyment and delight.

We have a creative God who has given us above and beyond

even that which we could imagine.

We have so much to be thankful for.

23rd August

———————————

Belief in God is not a sign of weakness.

It is a realisation that we are not the most powerful,

most intelligent or the most important thing in this life.

24th August

———————————

Create for yourself an environment in which to grow.

What is it in your life that is stopping you

from growing closer to God?

Are you too busy, distracted or tired?

Is something or someone constantly dragging you

away from spending time with Him?

Dare I suggest unconfessed sin or wrong attitudes?

Perhaps now is the time to sort those things out?

What could you put in place to help you draw nearer to God?

What would help you?

A regular time to pray?

A house group?

A prayer triplet?

Bible reading notes?

A mentor?

What bad habits are you going to break,

and what good habits will you choose to get into

from this day forward?

What are you going to do to create for yourself

an environment in which to grow?

25th August

_____

However far we fall,

God's arms are always there to catch us.

His hands are there to pick us up,

and His grace is there to restore us.

26th August

_____

It's not the strength of your faith that counts

or the level of your theological comprehension.

It's not your discipline in reading your Bible

or remembering to pray.

It's not even your good deeds or the depth of your character.

What counts is the unbelievable, overwhelming,

unsurpassed and amazing grace of God.

27th August

_____

God's light shines into our lives.

We have the choice to live in that light

or hide in the shadow it creates.

28th August

_____

One thing that is great to develop and frustrates the devil

and our enemies no end is bounce-back-ability.

God loves us to bounce back from whatever life throws at us,

and if we hold onto His hand, we bounce back much quicker.

29th August

Your worth is not to be found in your job title,

your wealth or your social standing.

It is not to be measured by the number of friends you have

or even by what people think of you.

Your true worth can only be measured

by the unconditional love that God has for you,

His willingness to adopt you into His family

and in His sending His only son to die for you.

When we see what God really thinks of us,

how much He loves us and how much He has done for us,

we can then see that our worth is truly beyond measure.

30th August

Nothing but an unreserved acceptance that Jesus Christ

paid the ultimate price for our

relationship to be restored with God will suffice.

No works will ever be enough.

No excuses will ever do.

There is nothing we can bring to the bargaining table

except Christ himself, on our behalf.

Simple acceptance paves the way –

not I Lord, but what You have done for me.

31st August

———————————

Christianity without love is no more than just religion.

September

1st September

———————————

The darkest of nights cannot extinguish the smallest of lights.

Jesus within us will shine brightly if we allow ourselves to be the

lantern through which the world can see Him.

2nd September

———————————

Never forget to be thankful for all your friends.

A good friend is a true gift from God.

Who will you be a good friend to this week?

3rd September

———————————

God loves the ugly, the broken, the downhearted,

the hopeless, the helpless, and the homeless.

God loves the unlovely, the awkward,

the anxious, and the unruly.

God loves the difficult, the dirty, the ordinary and the average.

No-one is beyond the all-encompassing love of God.

4th September

———————————

We are the church!

You and I are the church.

The building we meet in on a Sunday is not the Church.

We are the church gathered on a Sunday,

and also you and I are the church at home,

at work, and at the shops.

Wherever we go, we are the church.

You cannot go to church

because wherever you go, you are church.

The church is people.

The church reaches out into the community

if you are in the community.

Does the church have a presence in the school

or local business?

It does if we are there.

Wherever you go, the church is there.

Wherever you go, you are a representative of Jesus Christ.

How is the church going to be seen today?

How is the church going to meet the

needs of those it comes across today?

How is the church going to serve the local community?

5th September

_____

God loves to make the uncomfortable, comfortable.

He loves to bring order out of chaos

and bring a little chaos to our order.

God is always the same, but never predictable.

He is strong and mighty, and at the same time,

gentle and caring.

He is fast to act, yet slow to anger.

He is all-encompassing, yet intimate and personable.

No wonder He is indescribable!

6th September

_____

On the 7th Day, God stopped creating.

He did not, however, just stop.

Not for one single day has God stopped loving,

sustaining and caring for His creation.

God loves you 24/7 from before you were born and into eternity!

7th September

_____

Only the stuff in your life that you feed, will grow.

What will you be feeding today?

8th September

_____

What is the Good News?

Do we really believe that the News is Good?

Do our lives live out the fact that we have found

the answers to many of life's big questions?

Do we live like we've truly been rescued from the jaws of death?

Moreover, do people see in us the Good News?

Do we show others more Christ or criticism?

If they look at us, do they see Jehovah or judgement?

Do people see in us a glimpse of heaven or just hypocrisy?

Our lives are the Gospel message

through which people can find Christ.

What will our lives say to those around us today?

9th September

─────────────

When was the last time you went to Jesus,

washed His feet with your tears, dried them

with your hair and dressed his feet

with the most expensive things you had?

10th September

─────────────

Never let a point of theology,

however strongly you believe it

or however profoundly it affects your life,

get in the way of the love you hold for one another.

11th September

─────────────

Prayer is the refocusing of our lives

on who and what is most important.

It is acknowledging who is in charge and what we owe Him.

It's about giving the glory back!

12th September

_____

The God that I worship can still the waves and calm the storm

and yet, in His wisdom, allows me to endure them

so that I may become stronger and wiser

and a little bit more like Him.

13th September

_____

I went to a thanksgiving service yesterday for a wonderful lady.

She impacted many people around the world,

not because of what she said or even what she did,

but because of who she was.

What better legacy can someone leave?

14th September

———————————

If you honour Him with your life,

God will honour you in your death!

15th September

———————————

Christ alone is my salvation

Christ alone is my reward

Christ beside me

Christ before me

Christ within me

Christ is Lord

16th September

———————————

God is by your side, constantly waiting.

He is waiting for you to converse with Him.

He is waiting for you to acknowledge your need of Him.

He is waiting to fill you afresh.

He is waiting to wrap you in His love.

He is waiting to reassure you and comfort you.

He is waiting for you to listen to Him.

He is waiting to be all that you need of Him.

He is waiting for you to rest in His presence.

God is always waiting.

Will you make Him wait much longer?

17th September

——————————

We can know God as a mighty creator;

We can study God as an historical figure;

We can understand God as a King,

a ruler and a figure of supreme authority.

We can comprehend that God is a judge,

a lawgiver and a great High Priest;

but it is only through God's Spirit

that we can know him as ABBA, Father...

Daddy!

18th September

———————————

God's grace is more than sufficient

God's mercy is unfathomable

God's love is unconditional

God's patience is never-ending

God's peace is more profound than we'll ever know

God's power is inexhaustible

God's reliability is unquestionable

God's goodness and kindness are unquenchable

All of this for you, and much more besides!

It kind of blows your mind, doesn't it?

19th September

———————————

Not for our glory Lord, but for your glory –

take our lives and use them as you choose.

20th September

———————————

We must remember to praise God when the sun is shining

AND when the storm is blowing!

If God is worthy of our praise,

He is worthy of it no matter our circumstances!

21st September

_____

Our lives need to be lived in conversation with God.

22nd September

_____

We can believe without having all the answers.

We can trust God without understanding everything.

We can follow without having to know where we are being led.

We can know God is near to us without feeling it.

We can serve God without knowing it.

But we cannot hear God without listening.

We cannot follow God with trying.

We cannot know God through anyone but Jesus,

His Word and His Spirit.

23rd September

When God is all you have, God is all you need!

24th September

Jesus returned to His Father so that

He could no longer be with us but in us!

25th September

If we are truly open to God speaking to us,

He can speak through anything!

26th September

Our image of God is vitally important to us in our Christian life!

How we see Him will directly affect how we relate to Him,

how we do what He asks of us and how we see ourselves.

Do we see Him as a dictator God

just waiting for us to do wrong so that He can punish us?

Do we see Him as a distant, powerless God

who is disinterested in us?

Or, do we see Him as a loving father,

involved, caring, able to protect and help, and wanting

the best for us in all situations?

Our image of God goes hand in hand with another vital aspect

– what do we believe about how God sees us?

Do we think God sees us as pawns to be played with?

How about people to be controlled and subdued?

Does He view us with contempt, anger and frustration?

Does He see us as His children?

As the apple of His eye?

As the pinnacle of his creation?

What we believe about God

and what we believe He thinks about us

will shape our lives more than anything else.

27th September

_____

When we go on a trip, my youngest's favourite phrase,

as with many young ones, is "are we nearly there yet?"

Now I don't have a satisfying answer to give him

that he can understand!

According to the sat nav,

I could tell him that we'll be there in 4 hours

or it's another 289 miles,

but he would have no comprehension of what that meant!

The same is true of us and God!

We have many questions for God...

What about suffering?

Does hell really exist,

and how can a God of love send people there?

Why did my husband, child, dad have to die?

When are you coming back?

Why do evil people seem to get away with it?

The list could go on and on!

However, the truth is, we could not comprehend the answers

that God would give; to us, they would make no sense!

Our brains are simply not developed enough

to take in the answers!

Sometimes we just have to sit back and trust

that we can't understand everything and

trust God, who has all the answers

even if we'll never comprehend them.

28th September

_____

Whatever you speak into the lives of those

around you will rise up in them!

So, if you focus on their sin, that will rise up in them.

However, if you speak of their potential,

it will be that potential that grows!

If we speak to them of their lack or their failings,

it will be that that rises up; but if we speak

of the security they can find in God, His love for them,

their importance to Him, it will be that that rises up!

We need to be very careful how we talk to people,

what we talk about and how we speak

God into their lives!

29th September

_____

We live in an ever-changing world!

It is frightening how much change we experience.

However, God is changeless, unchanging, constant, and stable.

We know change, we know chaos and flux

– do we really know Him who is changeless and

the security and comfort to be found in Him?

30th September

_____

We cannot give to God; we can only give back to God!

October

1st October

_____

Prayer is for us to ask God for things that

will enhance our relationship with Him!

2nd October

_____

God not only wants the best for you in all circumstances,

but He also has the ability to provide the

best for you in all circumstances!

3rd October

_____

Sometimes we need God's grace and mercy; sometimes,

we need to show God's grace and mercy!

4th October

_____

How do I pray?

Pray as if Jesus just turned up on your doorstep!!

Pray as you would talk to him

if you had just met him face to face!

We tend to pray as if He was a big agony aunt in the sky,

there to solve all our problems,

hear our worries and give us what we need.

However, I would hope if Jesus turned up on my doorstep,

I would start with praising Him, continue in thanking Him.

I would want to spend time listening

to what He wanted to say to me.

Then, just as He was walking out the door,

if I were brave enough,

I might just ask him for something.

5th October

_____

In life, people will always come along and hurt you.

You have the choice though,

to let that hurt linger in your life or whether you will give it to

God, forgive and move on.

The choice is yours;

people can only hurt you as much as you let them!

6th October

―――――――――

In its best form,

Prayer is seeking what God wants to do

and then asking Him to do it!

7th October

―――――――――

Truth is something to be highly prized!

People have fought and died for it!

People have spent their lives unwrapping it

so we could understand it!

People have held onto it

through the most difficult of circumstances!

It is truth that has given the weak, strength

and the powerless true power!

We must treasure it,

protect it and most of all, share it for the good of all!

Will you share the truth of God today?

8th October

_____

Jesus' ministry started from a position of security!

God told Jesus that

"You are my Son, whom I love, with you I am well pleased!"

This took place before Jesus had taught, healed,

discipled, performed miracles, etc.

God loved Him and was pleased with Him for who He was

and not for what He had done.

The great thing is...

the same is true for us.

God loves us for who we are, faults and all,

not for what we have done for Him!!

We can start each day from a place of security,

knowing we are loved, valued, appreciated,

special, wanted and important to God.

9th October

_____

God has unconditional love for each and every one of us!

A love that is unchanging, constant, and never-ending.

We must develop this love for those around us.

A love that covers over differences and disagreements.

A love that always forgives, is full of grace and mercy.

A love that focuses on that which unites,

not that which divides.

A love that picks up the fallen and reinstates them.

A love that puts others first.

A love that focuses on the goal

but ensures we don't step on others to get there.

We need to develop a Christ-like love

that would go all the way to the cross if required

and ensures that all whom we met along the way

would either mourn or celebrate when we got there!

10th October

_____

God's grace is more than sufficient for you, yes, even you.

It is a radical, extravagant, overwhelming gift

that requires only that we accept it!

11th October

———————————

What do our words and actions say as church?

Our words say we are church 24/7;

our actions say church is for Sunday

and maybe once during the week!

Our words say church is one of the only organisations

devoted to the benefit of its non-members;

our actions say we look after ourselves

(and not always very well!).

Our words say we give everything to you Lord;

our actions say 10 percent of our money

and even less of our time.

I could go on, but isn't it about time we bridged the gap

between our words and actions?

12th October

———————————

Jesus may not want us to literally cut off our hands

or feet or gouge out our eyes, but what

is He calling us to get rid of in our lives

that is keeping us from Him?

13th October

_____

Some things in life just don't make sense – it's a fact!

We can either spend our time worrying about them

or marvelling in the mystery of God's

wonderful creation –

which we fully acknowledge is way beyond

the realms of our comprehension!

The choice is ours.

Will we worry that we don't understand some things,

or praise God that He does?

14th October

_____

Whatever you turn your hand to,

do it in God's strength and for His glory!

15th October

_____

God may simply be asking you to speak His love into the life

of another today with a heartfelt smile.

It could completely turn their day around!

16th October

_____

Sometimes,

when you show people a little of God's mercy

through your words or actions,

you will need to show it again and again

before they will understand it,

accept it and benefit from it!

17th October

_____

We all have so much to be thankful for!!

However, it doesn't always feel that way,

and sometimes everything feels simply naff!

Lord, when life seems this way, please help us to react well!

Help us to have the attitude...

Even though I feel like this, I WILL praise the Lord.

Even though everything seems to be going wrong,

I WILL give thanks to God.

Even though the Lord seems far away,

I WILL remember that He is right by my side.

18th October

————————————

Don't be too hard on yourself!

Always remember that God loves you exactly as you are

with all your faults and failures.

That unconditional love that He has for us

should drive us to be better,

not guilt or laws or our conscience!

19th October

————————————

Sometimes God calls us away from situations

that He once called us to!

It takes strength and wisdom to walk away.

Lord, grant us that strength and wisdom in such situations!

Help us to leave in the best possible way.

Help us to know for sure that it is Your will!

20th October

————————————

There is a hunger deep within the hearts of humankind

that can only be met by a relationship with Jesus Christ!

Some try to feed this hunger with drugs,

sex, adrenalin-fuelled activities,

work, sport and so on, but they never really satisfy!

The more we feast on these things, the more we want!

Jesus Christ is the only person who is sufficient!

21st October

————————————

If you are a Christian, you are a follower of Christ!

If you only follow Him on a Sunday,

from time to time or just when it suits you, you will

soon find you've lost Him

and to follow Him again will take much searching.

If you seek Him, you will find Him, but it may take a while.

If you follow Him day by day,

step by step, you will always know where He is!

Don't wait for an emergency to seek Him!

22nd October

_____

Sometimes you have to close, lock

and throw away the key to one door

before God opens a much better door for you!

23rd October

_____

What is church?

It is a group of people who hold each other in their hearts!

(among other things!)

24th October

―――――――――

Nothing we can ever do will be enough; however,

God's grace is more than sufficient to make up for our lack!

25th October

―――――――――

It's through the brokenness and the cracks in our lives

that God shines in and through!

26th October

―――――――――

Let your worries turn you to prayer, not to more worry!

27th October

―――――――――

A toe is such a tiny part of the body but damaging just one toe

affects the body in so many different ways.

The same is true of sin in our lives,

it may just seem like something minor, but it affects our

lives and those around us in so many different

and dangerous ways.

28th October

_____

Trust God to transform your life.

Live with expectancy.

Pray with belief.

Hope with Faith.

Live in the Spirit.

Dwell in His word.

Act in honesty and integrity.

Become transformed.

29th October

_____

Are you willing to be a hero?

Have you ever considered that one of the problems

with the Western Church is that it has

a few saints but not any real heroes?

Who is there for people to look up to in the church today?

Whom do we emulate?

Where are the Davids to fight the Goliaths that surround us?

Where are the Noahs to build us Arks to stop us drowning?

Where are the Abrahams, Josephs, Stephens, Johns?

Are you willing to step up to the plate

and be a hero for this generation?

30th October

———————————

Putting your trust in God is like giving yourself an anchor,

a life jacket and an emergency radio all rolled into one!

31st October

———————————

You never know what today's journey may bring,

but with a map (the Bible), a compass

(the Holy Spirit) and a willingness to engage with them,

you won't go far wrong!

November

When we fail to understand one another,

God calls us to a deep respect for, not only the

other person's point of view, but more importantly,

a deep respect and love for the other person.

In all things, remember that we are all more important

than our opinions and others are always more important,

to God and us, than what they do or say!

1st November

2nd November

It is only in remembering the person behind the words

that their real meaning can be understood.

Let us take time to truly understand each other and God,

remembering that all words from God will encourage, build-up,

affirm, strengthen and remind us of His love.

3rd November

Sometimes when the storms of life are raging around us,

we have the faith, strength and courage

to step out of the boat and walk on water.

At other times when the waves are tossing us here,

there, and everywhere we just need to find a calm harbour,

get out of the boat, return to dry land

and trust God that the storm will pass.

4th November

Sometimes, there is a pain, a sadness or sorrow you feel

that only God can understand.

Everyone may try and sympathise,

but only God can empathise.

Speak to Him about it,

pour out your heart to Him

for He longs to help you with your burdens.

5th November

_____

Let everything you do today

bring glory to the one who made you

and breathed His life into you so

that you can do everything you're going to do today!

6th November

_____

Jesus came to earth, giving up everything.

On earth, He poured himself out as a sacrifice

for all the wrong we would ever do.

He reconciled us to God in the only possible way,

by dying for us.

He gave His all for us.

What will we give up for Him today?

7th November

_____

I choose to rejoice and be thankful in all my circumstances.

Whether I feel happy or sad, angry,

frustrated or on top of the world.

I will rejoice because I really do have so much

to be thankful to God for.

8th November

———————————————

Give what you can.

Take what you need.

Ask God for what you don't have.

Trust friends for the hard times.

Be a great friend in the good times.

Pray for those you know who are in need.

Give thanks for all that God has given you.

9th November

———————————————

In our darkest times, God is closest to us.

We may not feel His presence, but He is there.

He is our guide and our staff.

He is a light to our feet and a strength to our bones.

He will NEVER let us down!

We have the choice to follow in His ways,

to walk with Him in the garden or walk away

when the going gets tough.

However, we will soon find that the going is never

more formidable than when we choose

to walk away from God's desire for our life!

10th November

———————————

Sometimes, we just need to do what is right in the eyes of God

and let Him deal with all the fallout!

11th November

———————————

What is your Christian ambition?

What do you want to attempt for God?

What are you going to ask God to help you achieve?

What is your holy five-year plan?

What do you need to put right this year

that has been wrong for a while?

How are you going to draw nearer to God

in the next 12 months?

What is your strategy for doing this?

I challenge you over the next few weeks

to seek God over these things, and let's move

forward together into a closer,

more productive, relationship with God!

12th November

_____

What's done is done, and there is very little we can do about it

other than place it into the hands of God and leave it there,

trusting that He will deal with it in the best possible,

most just, way.

13th November

_____

Sin not only separates us from God;

it separates us from one another

and all the riches that there are to be found in Christ.

However, we have an option –

we can turn away from our sin,

receive full forgiveness through the grace and mercy of God

in Christ Jesus and move back into good relationship

with God.

Will you trust Him with your future

and turn your back on that which is wrong in your life?

14th November

———————————

God brings clarity out of confusion.

He brings order out of chaos.

He comes to make the wealthy poor and the poor rich.

He makes the comfortable uncomfortable

and the uncomfortable comfortable.

He makes the intelligent seem like fools

and children appear wise.

Our strengths can be barriers to God,

but He uses our weaknesses as His strengths.

15th November

———————————

God has promised that He will never leave us.

Therefore, God is always with us

whether we can feel His presence or not.

God has said it; therefore it is so!

16th November

———————————

What or who are you going to allow to rule in your life today?

Is it going to be God, Jesus and the Holy Spirit?

Or is it going to be your circumstances,

other people, past, mistakes, doubts, or fears?

The choice is yours!

17th November

———————————

Don't praise God when the sun shines

if you're not prepared to praise Him

also when the storms come!

18th November

———————————

God asks us to forgive one another.

In forgiving, we release ourselves from the bonds of

disobedience, bitterness, hatred and anger.

19th November

———————————

God is amazing all the time!

God is good, kind, compassionate, faithful,

and trustworthy every minute of every day.

When things are going badly, when people die,

when our heart aches, when we feel down –

God is still just as good and amazing.

We may not feel that way about Him,

but that doesn't change the reality.

Celebrate today a God who is constant,

never changing and totally AMAZING!

20th November

God does not want you to be defined by your past mistakes.

He wants you to be forgiven,

released from them, and able to move on.

21st November

Count yourself lucky, how happy you must be

— you get a fresh start, your slate's wiped clean.

Count yourself lucky—

God holds nothing against you,

and you're holding nothing back from him.

When I kept it all inside, my bones turned to powder;

my words became daylong groans.

The pressure never let up;

all the juices of my life dried up.

Then I let it all out; I said,

"I'll make a clean breast of my failures to God."

Suddenly the pressure was gone.

My guilt dissolved, my sin disappeared.

These things add up.

Every one of us needs to pray.

When all hell breaks loose and the dam bursts,

then we'll be on high ground, untouched.

God's my island hideaway.

He keeps danger far from the shore,

throws garlands of hosannas around my neck.

Let me give you some good advice.

I'm looking you in the eye and giving it to you straight:

"Don't be stubborn like a horse or mule

that needs bit and bridle to stay on track."

God-defiers are always in trouble.

God-affirmers find themselves loved

every time they turn around.

Celebrate God.

Sing together—everyone!

All your honest hearts raise the roof!

22nd November

———————————

If you do what is right in the eyes of God,

He will honour you, prepare a way for you

and will never let you down.

Doing the right thing isn't always easy,

but it is always the best thing for you to do.

God knows your struggles,

but He also holds the keys to your solutions.

He will lead you, and if you follow Him,

there you will find His love, peace and joy!

When you are in darkness,

God provides the light to lead you out.

Will you follow Him today?

23rd November

_____

God loves to use the brokenness of our lives,

the rubbish, the dross, the mistakes

and the ashes to build something new and beautiful.

24th November

_____

Sometimes the pain we feel for a situation

is a small reminder of how God's heart breaks

for all his world.

25th November

———————————————

Be still.

Stop.

Quieten yourself.

Rest awhile.

Still your heart and clear your mind.

Put all distractions to one side.

Now, focus on God

and know that He is who He says He is.

26th November

———————————————

God is a jealous God who wants our all.

He wants our complete attention,

our total devotion and our whole heart!

He doesn't want to share us with anything.

27th November

When God asks us to pick up our cross daily,

it is not a call to suffering, pain, and death.

It is, in fact, a call to perspective and focus.

Picking up our cross

(notice not picking up the cross of Christ, but our cross)

focuses us on the immediate future and our impending death.

Our focus becomes what needs to get done before we die.

Our focus has an urgency to it!

How differently would we live our lives

if we knew we were going to die next week?

A person carrying their cross knows

they only have a short time to live, a short time to

make their peace with those around them

and a short time to think about the more

significant issues of life.

Do we need that kind of focus now?

28th November

Do not let your life be ruled by your emotions or feelings,

but by truth and wisdom.

Your feelings will often misguide you and confuse you.

If I go outside on a sunny but windy day,

I may not feel the heat of the sun.

If I follow my feelings, I get burnt.

If I follow truth, I remain safe.

I may not always feel the love of God,

but it is always there.

If I follow my feelings,

I will feel unloved at times.

If I follow truth,

I will know God's love for me every second of every day!

29th November

———————————

We often talk about the cost of discipleship.

We think of how much being a Christian is going to cost us.

However, the real question we need to ask

is how much NOT being a Disciple of Christ will cost us!

30th November

_____

What would Jesus do today if He were you?

December

———————————

Whatever road you have to travel, He is by your side.

Whatever pain you have to bear, He knows how you feel.

Whatever your fears or worries are about,

He is holding you, protecting you, and is with you in them.

Whatever griefs you have, He is mourning with you.

Whatever you are going through,

God is the only one who can genuinely empathise with you.

Talk to Him about it.

He longs to help and carry you in your troubles.

2nd December

———————————

God believes in good relationship.

He knows that good relationships are worth fighting for.

He knows that strong relationships require hard work.

He knows that the best relationships

are ones that have been tried and tested.

Thank you, Lord, for the gift of relationship!

3rd December

_____

God is good!

No matter your circumstances,

however you feel, God is good!

Whether He answers your prayers in the way you want

or doesn't seem to answer them at all,

God is still good!

Whether you are happy, mourning, depressed, hopeless,

failing, dying, or in pain or despair,

God is still Good!

4th December

_____

What we believe about God

is one of the most essential things in life.

Whom we believe He is and what we believe He thinks about us

are huge things.

They will shape most other things

and influence most things we do.

They will help form how we feel about others and ourselves

and how we relate to those around us.

Have you recently considered what you believe about Him?

5th December

———————————

If we want to be effective as Christians,

we need to learn to live, not in the present past,

but in the present future!

6th December

———————————

God doesn't love you because you are good or nice –

He loves you because He is good and nice!

7th December

———————————

What idols do you need to rid your life of?

What do you spend too much time doing?

What is your daily focus?

What idols does your church have?

Does your church spend a bit too much time

focusing on money, business, buildings, the

future, the past or any host of other things that are not healthy?

Are you and your church managing to put the first things first?

Is God your proper focus or just an added extra?

Are you prepared to change?

Your idols may not be made of gold or silver,

but they will still get in the way of your

relationship with God.

Let us all have the courage to look at our lives honestly

and change those things that need to be changed.

8th December

_____

When life is confusing, daunting or frightening,

we must remember that we can stand firm

upon the Rock.

We have a solid foundation,

even if it doesn't always feel that way.

God will prevent us from stumbling.

He will stand by our side through good times and bad.

He will provide light for our path.

He will lift up the fallen and restore them.

When things are tough, seek out all that God has to offer.

He will shelter us under His wing and lead us on.

9th December

———————————

If you are a friend of mine, close or not,

what you do matters not to me.

If you are kind and generous, I thank God for you.

If you are rude to me and hurt me,

I forgive you and ask God to be with you in your struggle.

It does not matter whether you are rich or poor,

what job you have, what positions you hold,

what gifts and skills you have

or whether you have letters after your name.

I care not if you are black or white, straight or gay,

employed or unemployable, educated or uneducated,

a murderer or a monk.

I do not judge you.

If you are a friend of mine,

I am proud to call you my friend.

I thank God for you and pray that He would bless you,

guide you and protect you.

Thank you for being my friend!

10th December

––––––––––––––

Everything that we give to God,

He can use for His glory.

Be it time, money, our homes, skills, our minds or whatever –

God can use all to build His heavenly kingdom here on earth.

11th December

––––––––––––––

The Christian journey is a journey in company.

God, the Holy Spirit, walks alongside us,

and God has placed us in families,

friendship groups and churches.

We are there for one another, to encourage, build up and guide

Will you humble yourself

and rely on those God has put around you?

Will you also be there for them?

12th December

If we are only prepared to surrender part of our life to God,

we miss out on God working in our whole life.

It is usually the area that we fail to surrender

that needs God's touch the most.

Don't hold anything back.

God desires our all,

and we need everything that God has to offer.

13th December

You can fool all of the people some of the time

and some of the people all of the time,

but don't be fooled into believing that you can fool yourself

and certainly don't be fooled into believing

that you can fool God.

14th December

———————————

There is true freedom for people who place their trust in God.

When we trust Him, our fears fade, and our faith grows.

When we truly trust God, He will NEVER let us down.

15th December

———————————

When God has your whole heart,

it begins to beat as His heart does.

You begin to see things in the way God does.

You begin to love as He loves

and have compassion as He has compassion.

When God has your heart, you become more like Him.

When you give God your whole heart,

He lovingly mends it and sets its rhythm.

God becomes your pace-maker.

Are you brave enough to give God your whole heart?

16th December

It's never too late to start the rest of your life over again.

God is the God of second chances –

always more willing to forgive

than we are willing to ask for forgiveness.

He loves to give us a clean sheet –

even though He knows full well

that we'll mess it up all over again!

17th December

It is when we look to the Trinity that we see the best example

of community working in perfect harmony.

18th December

When things don't go to plan,

you have to wonder if they were God's plans

or your plans in the first place!

19th December

Being there is sometimes all God asks us to do.

We sometimes don't need words or the proper insight;

we just need to be there for someone.

Our presence, like God's presence,

is sometimes all that is needed.

20th December

If God has spoken into a situation, hold firm to that.

Don't give up.

Don't let circumstances

or other people persuade you otherwise.

Don't let practicalities get in the way

of what God is asking you to do.

It may seem impossible but, if God has called you to it,

He will provide a way through.

21st December

———————————

Christ is our rock and our foundation.

He is solid, secure, trustworthy, and He never changes.

He is dependable, faithful and always there for us.

If we build our lives on Him, we will stand firm.

The storms of life may shake us, but we will not fall.

The waves may lap around our ankles, but we will not drown.

22nd December

———————————

Whatever we feed in our lives grows.

Whatever we starve in our lives dies.

Let us learn to feed the Holy Spirit,

feed our faith, feed all that is good.

Let us persevere in starving all sin

and everything in our lives that is bad.

Lord, give us the strength to do this

and the wisdom to know which is which.

23rd December

———————————

Be encouraged; God is at work –

He is speaking, He is present.

He is no distant God that once came near.

He is not a God that spoke once and now is silent –

He is here; He is speaking; He is at work!

24th December

———————————

Making yourself vulnerable before someone

puts a weapon in their hand.

A weapon that they can use to harm you

or protect, defend and grow you.

If you are ever given that weapon, use it wisely,

in a Godly way – for any wounds you inflict

will scar you and Christ just as much!

25th December

———————————

The more points of connection the family of God can have,

the stronger it will be.

It is in relationship with one another

that our strength as church grows.

26th December

————————————

What is worship if it is not our heart's response

to who God is and what He has done?

27th December

————————————

The greatest gift we can give to someone

is to faithfully pray for them –

lifting them up to the throne of grace

and seeking God's input into their lives.

28th December

————————————

It is in relationship with others

that we find out much about ourselves.

It is in relationship with God

that we find out who we really are.

29th December

————————————

Being a Christian is not a one-off decision

to put your faith in God;

it is a daily decision

to pick up your cross

and follow wherever He may lead!

30th December

————————————

It is in becoming vulnerable before God

and His people that we lay the firmest foundation

for us to become strong.

31st December

————————————

We wouldn't really want to be anybody else,

but sometimes, perhaps we should strive to

be a better version of ourselves.

A more "Jesus-like" version of ourselves.

I hope you have enjoyed and benefited from the thoughts I have shared in this book. If so, please consider leaving a review because this helps others decide if it is a book worth reading. Please leave a review by searching for the book on Amazon and scrolling down to the review section; I would so much appreciate this.

If you would like a free copy of my book
of Modern Prayers or would like to sign up
for information on future promotions,
new books or special offers,
please scan the QR code below
or visit my websitewww.nathan-haddock-books.co.uk

Other books by Nathan Haddock

God's Solution to Worry, Anxiety, and Fear

Come Pray With Me

Gathered Together Under His Wing (Christian Poetry)

For more information, please visit my website

www.nathan-haddock-books.co.uk

or feel free to e-mail me

mailto:nathan@nathan-haddock-books.co.uk

Printed in Great Britain
by Amazon

15772715R00112